TEST YOURSELF ON THESE QUE........
HOW MUCH YOU KNOW ABOUT YOUR BELOVED
TEAM LIVERPOOL FC.

THESE QUESTIONS HAVE BEEN DRAWN UP FROM
A WIDE RANGE OF TOPICS WHICH INCLUDE CLUB
HISTORY, PLAYERS HISTORY, COMPETITION
STATISTICS, APPEARANCES, SEASON STATISTICS,
AND SEVERAL OTHER TOPICS.

THE OPTIONS ARE LETTERED A TO C WITH ANY ONE
OF THEM BEING THE RIGHT ANSWER. TO MAKE THE MOST
OUT OF THE QUIZ, MAKE SURE TO READ THE QUESTIONS
OVER AGAIN TO AVOID PICKING THE WRONG ANSWER.
THE DIFFERENCE BETWEEN THE RIGHT AND WRONG
ANSWER CAN BE IN A WORD IN A 'NOT' OR 'IN'.

MANY COMPETITIONS HAVE BEEN MENTIONED HERE,
WITH SOME QUESTIONS ARE COMPETITION-SPECIFIC.

FOR EXAMPLE, SOME QUESTIONS ARE PREMIER LEAGUE
SPECIFIC WHILE SOME ARE IN THE LEAGUE GENERALLY.
SOME QUESTIONS ARE UEFA CHAMPIONS LEAGUE
SPECIFIC, WHILE OTHERS SPEAK OF EUROPE IN GENERAL.

TAKE NOTE TO DISTINGUISH WHICH
COMPETITION THE QUESTION IS FOCUSED ON.

PREMIER LEAGUE OR PL TALKS ABOUT THE PERIOD FROM
THE 1992/1993 SEASON IN THE ENGLISH LEAGUE.

EUROPE TALKS ABOUT ALL CONTINENTAL COMPETITIONS.

LEAGUE OR TOP-FLIGHT TALKS ABOUT THE LEAGUE
GENERALLY FROM ITS INCEPTION TILL CURRENT
PREMIER LEAGUE FORMAT.

GOODLUCK.

WHO WAS THE FIRST LIVERPOOL PLAYER TO MISS A PENALTY?

A.   IAN RUSH

B.   GEORGE ALLAN

C.   FRANK BECTON

WHICH TEAM DID LIVERPOOL WIN IN THE SEMI-FINAL OF THE 2005 CHAMPIONS LEAGUE ON THEIR WAY TO THE FINAL?

A.   JUVENTUS

B.   OLYMPIAKOS

C.   CHELSEA

WHO HAS THE RECORD OF THE QUICKEST HAT-TRICK IN LIVERPOOL HISTORY?

A.   ROBBIE FOWLER

B.   SADIO MANE

C.   MOHAMED SALAH

PLAYER WITH THE MOST HAT-TRICKS FOR LIVERPOOL IN A SINGLE SEASON FOR LIVERPOOL

A.   ROBBIE FOWLER

B.   ROGER HUNT

C.   LIUS SUAREZ

WHO IS LIVERPOOL'S LONGEST-SERVING PLAYER BY NUMBER OF YEARS?

A.   ELISHA SCOTT

B.   ROGER HUNT

C.   JAMIE CARRAGHER

WHO WAS THE FIRST PLAYER TO SCORE FOR LIVERPOOL?

A.   GEORGE ALLAN

B.   BILL SHANKLY

C.   MALCOLM MCVEAN

MOST USED SUBSTITUTE FOR LIVERPOOL IN THE PL

A.   RYAN BABEL

B.   LUCAS LEIVA

C.   MAXI RODRIGUEZ

KEEPER WITH MOST PENALTY SAVES FOR LIVERPOOL

A.   BRUCE GROBBELAAR

B.   SIMON MIGNOLET

C.   SAM HARDY

HOW MANY TIMES WAS LUCAS LEIVA SENT OFF FOR LIVERPOOL?

A.   3

B.   2

C.   4

KEEPER WITH MOST PENALTY SAVES FOR LIVERPOOL

A.   BRUCE GROBBELAAR

B.   SIMON MIGNOLET

C.   SAM HARDY

QUESTION 11

REFEREE TO HAVE OFFICIATED THE MOST GAMES FOR LIVERPOOL

A.   MICHAEL OLIVER

B.   HOWARD WEBB

C.   MARTIN ATKINSON

QUESTION 12

PLAYER WITH MOST GOALS IN A SINGLE GAME FOR LIVERPOOL

A.   MOHAMED SALAH

B.   IAN RUSH

C.   LUIS SUAREZ

QUESTION 13

TWO PLAYERS HAVE SCORED FOUR GOALS IN A SINGLE MATCH AGAINST LIVERPOOL

A. MARK VIDUKA
ANDY COLE

B. ANDREY ARSHAVIN
JIMMY HASSELBAINK

C. MARK VIDUKA
ANDREY ARSHAVIN

QUESTION 14

PLAYER TO HAVE SCORED THE MOST GOAL AGAINST LIVERPOOL IN THE PL

A. ANDY COLE
B. THIERRY HENRY
C. WAYNE ROONEY

WHO WAS MORE EXPENSIVE?

A.   LUIZ SUAREZ
B.   ADAM LALLANA
C.   JORDAN HENDERSON

WHICH TEAM HAS LOST THE MOST AGAINST LIVERPOOL IN THE LEAGUE?

A.   ASTON VILLA
B.   EVERTON
C.   CRYSTAL PALACE

QUESTION 17

WHICH TEAM HAS BEATEN LIVERPOOL THE MOST IN THE LEAGUE?

A.   CHELSEA

B.   ARSENAL

C.   MANCHESTER UNITED

QUESTION 18

PLAYER WITH THE MOST STARTS IN THE PL FOR LIVERPOOL

A.   JAMIE CARRAGHER

B.   STEVEN GERRARD

C.   KENNY DALGLISH

QUESTION 19

WHICH MANAGER SIGNED JIM BEGLIN FOR LIVERPOOL?

A.   BOB PAISLEY

B.   KENNY DALGLISH

C.   BILL SHANKLY

QUESTION 20

ONE OF THESE PLAYERS HAS MORE THAN TWO GOALS FOR LIVERPOOL IN EUROPE

A.   CRAIG BELLAMY

B.   FERNANDO MORIENTES

C.   XABI ALONSO

FIRST OPPONENT TO LIVERPOOL IN EUROPE

A.   ANDERLECHT

B.   KNATTSPYRNUFÉLAG
       REYKJAVÍKUR

C.   COLOGNE

FIRST PLAYER TO SCORE FOR LIVERPOOL IN EUROPE

A.   ROGER HUNT

B.   PHIL CHISNALL

C.   GORDON WALLACE

WHO IS LIVERPOOL'S FIRST SENEGALESE PLAYER?

A.   SADIO MANE

B.   SALIF DIAO

C.   EL HAJI DIOUF

WHO WAS LIVERPOOL'S FIRST ASIAN PLAYER?

A.   TAKUMI MINAMINO

B.   SHINJI KAGAWA

C.   TOMMY LEE

HOW MANY MANAGERS HAVE MANAGED LIVERPOOL TO DATE
(BOTH FULL-TIME AND INTERIM)?

A.   35

B.   24

C.   18

IAN CALLAGHAN MADE OVER 700 APPEARANCES FOR LIVERPOOL. HOW MANY TIMES WAS HE BOOKED?

A.   ONCE

B.   THREE TIMES

C.   FIVE

WHAT IS THE LARGEST CROWD LIVERPOOL HAVE HAD IN A PRE-SEASON GAME?

A.   95,446

B.   89,050

C.   101,254

LIVERPOOL HAVE SCORED 21 GOALS IN FA CUP FINALS. HOW MANY WERE SCORED IN THE FIRST HALF?

A.   15

B.   2

C.   12

ONE OF THESE PLAYERS HAVE SCORED IN THE FIRST HALF OF FA CUP FINAL FOR LIVERPOOL

A.   STEVEN GERRARD

B.   CRAIG BELLAMY

C.   DJIBRIL CISSE

WHO SCORED LIVERPOOL'S QUICKEST GOAL IN A EUROPEAN TIE?

A.   STEVEN GERRARD

B.   PHILIPPE COUTINHO

C.   JOE COLE

WHO WAS THE FIRST LIVERPOOL PLAYER TO SCORE A HAT-TRICK IN THREE DIFFERENT COMPETITIONS IN THE SAME SEASON?

A.   JOHN WARK

B.   JOHN BARNES

C.   IAN RUSH

LFC FIRST NON-BRITISH MANAGER

A.   GERARD HOULLIER

B.   JURGEN KLOPP

C.   RAFA BENITEZ

QUESTION 33

THE ONLY PLAYER TO APPEAR FOR BOTH LIVERPOOL AND EVERTON IN MERSEYSIDE DERBIES IN THE SAME SEASON

A.   ABEL XAVIER

B.   SIMON PHILLIP

C.   CRAIG BELLAMY

QUESTION 34

WHO WAS LIVERPOOL'S FIRST GREEK PLAYER?

A.   KOSTAS TSIMIKAS

B.   SOTIRIOS KYRGIAKOS

C.   TAKUMI MINAMINO

WHO WAS BILL SHANKLY'S FIRST LFC SIGNING?

A.   SAMMY REID

B.   KEVIN LEWIS

C.   RON YEATS

MOST APPEARANCES FOR LIVERPOOL FC

A.   JAMIE CARRAGHER

B.   IAN CALLAGHAN

C.   STEVEN GERRARD

FIRST LIVERPOOL PLAYER TO BE KNIGHTED

A.   KENNY ROGERS

B.   KENNY DALGLISH

C.   ROGER HUNT

HOW MANY NATIONALITIES HAVE MANAGED LIVERPOOL TILL DATE?

A.   13

B.   8

C.   6

BOTH AS PLAYER AND MANAGER, HOW MANY LEAGUE TITLES DID KENNY DALGLISH WIN?

A.   6

B.   12

C.   9

LFC YOUNGEST EVER CAPTAIN

A.   CURTIS JONES

B.   STEVEN GERRARD

C.   BEN WOODBURN

FEWEST LEAGUE GOALS CONCEDED IN A SEASON BY LIVERPOOL

A.   16

B.   14

C.   8

MOST LEAGUE GOALS SCORED IN A SEASON FOR LIVERPOOL

A.   100

B.   102

C.   106

MOST GOALS SCORED IN A PREMIER LEAGUE SEASON

A.   101

B.   102

C.   99

MOST CONSECUTIVE LEAGUE MATCHES WITH A LIVERPOOL GOAL

A.   44

B.   36

C.   56

MOST LEAGUE GOALS
CONCEDED IN A SEASON

A.   5 5

B.   7 7

C.   9 7

FEWEST LEAGUE GOALS
SCORED IN A SEASON

A.   4 2

B.   3 9

C.   6 6

WHICH OF THESE PLAYERS HAVE SCORED THE MOST GOALS IN A SINGLE SEASON FOR LIVERPOOL IN EUROPE?

A.   STEVEN GERRARD

B.   IAN RUSH

C.   ROBERTO FIRMINO

PLAYER WITH THE MOST ASSIST IN A SINGLE EUROPEAN SEASON FOR LIVERPOOL

A.   JAMES MILNER

B.   STEVEN GERRARD

C.   ROBERTO FIRMINO

ONE OF THESE PLAYERS NEVER MISSED A PREMIER LEAGUE PENALTY FOR LIVERPOOL

A.   DANNY MURPHY

B.   JAMES MILNER

C.   DIRK KUYT

OLDEST PLAYER TO PAY IN THE PL FOR LIVERPOOL

A.   PAUL JONES

B.   SAMI HYYPIA

C.   GARY MCALLISTER

WHICH OF THESE PLAYERS HAS SCORED FOR LIVERPOOL ON EVERY DAY OF THE WEEK?

A.   MILNER

B.   TORRES

C.   BELLAMY

WHO IS LIVERPOOL'S OLDEST PREMIER LEAGUE DEBUTANT?

A.   PAUL JONES

B.   BRAD JONES

C.   GARY MCALLISTER

WHICH MANAGER HAS OVERSEEN THE MOST GAMES FOR LIVERPOOL?

A.   BOB PAISLEY

B.   TOM WATSON

C.   BILL SHANKLY

WHO IS LIVERPOOL'S LONGEST SERVING MANAGER BY NUMBER OF GAMES?

A.   BILL SHANKLY

B.   TOM WATSON

C.   KENNY DALGLISH

WHO IS LIVERPOOL'S LONGEST SERVING MANAGER BY NUMBER OF YEARS?

A.   BILL SHANKLY

B.   BOB PAISLEY

C.   TOM WATSON

WHO IS LIVERPOOL'S OLDEST GOAL SCORER EVER?

A.   SAMI HYYPIA

B.   BILLY LIDDELL

C.   GARY MCALLISTER

WHAT IS THE BIGGEST WIN RECORDED BY LIVERPOOL IN A EUROPEAN TIE?

A.   11-0 AGAINST STRØMSGODSET

B.   13-1 AGAINST COLOGNE

C.   8-1 AGAINST FC NARNIA

MOST CLEAN SHEETS IN A PREMIER LEAGUE SEASON FOR LIVERPOOL

A.   SIMON MIGNOLET

B.   ALLISON BECKER

C.   PEPE REINA

WHO SCORED LIVERPOOL'S FASTEST GOAL IN THE PREMIER LEAGUE?

A.   NABY KIETA

B.   FERNANDO TORRES

C.   MARTIN SKRTEL

DEFENDER WITH MOST GOALS IN THE PREMIER LEAGUE FOR LIVERPOOL

A.   JOHN ARNE RIISE

B.   MARTIN SKRTEL

C.   SAMI HYYPIA

LIVERPOOL PLAYER WITH THE MOST ALL-TIME ASSIST

A.   IAN RUSH

B.   STEVE MCMANAMAN

C.   STEVEN GERRARD

KEEPER WITH MOST CLEAN SHEETS IN LIVERPOOL HISTORY

A.   ELISHA SCOTT

B.   RAY CLEMENCE

C.   BRUCE GROBBELAAR

WHAT NATIONALITY WAS JERZEY DUDEK

A.   GERMAN

B.   ZIMBABWEAN

C.   POLISH

LIVERPOOL PLAYER THAT MISSED THE MOST SPOT KICKS IN HIS LIVERPOOL CAREER

A.   MICHAEL OWEN

B.   PHIL NEAL

C.   STEVEN GERRARD

LIVERPOOL PLAYER THAT SCORED THE MOST SPOT KICKS

A.   DANNY MURPHY

B.   STEVEN GERRARD

C.   MOHAMED SALAH

HOW MANY PLAYERS MADE THEIR FIRST TEAM DEBUT IN THE 2019/2020 SEASON

A.   23

B.   17

C.   20

WHICH PLAYER HAS WARMED THE BEST MOST IN LIVERPOOL HISTORY?

A.   DIEGO CAVALIERI

B.   ALBERTO MORENO

C.   BRAD JONES

RONNIE MORAN WAS NOT A LIVERPOOL

A.   CAPTAIN

B.   CARETAKER COACH

C.   OWNER

KEEPER THAT HAS SAVED THE MOST PENALTIES FOR LIVERPOOL

A.   TOM HARDY

B.   SIMON MIGNOLET

C.   RAY CLEMENCE

LIVERPOOL PLAYER WITH THE MOST ASSIST IN A SINGLE PREMIER LEAGUE SEASON

A.   TRENT ARNOLD

B.   STEVEN GERRARD

C.   STEVE MCMANAMAN

WHO AMONG THEM GOT TO 100 GOALS FASTER FOR LIVERPOOL?

A.   SAM RAYBOULD

B.   ROGER HUNT

C.   MOHAMED SALAH

WHICH TEAM DID LIVERPOOL BEAT TO WIN THE 2006 FA CUP FINAL?

A.   SOUTHAMPTON

B.   CARDIFF CITY

C.   WEST HAM UNITED

HOW DID LIVERPOOL WIN CARDIFF IN THE 2012 CARLING CUP FINAL?

A.   PENALTY SHOOTOUT

B.   LONG-RANGE STEVEN GERRARD STRIKE

C.   LAST MINUTE DANIEL AGGER HEADER

AGAINST WHICH TEAM DID LIVERPOOL FIELD THEIR YOUNGEST IX IN THE PREMIER LEAGUE?

A.   SWANSEA

B.   WEST HAM UNITED

C.   WEST BROMWICH ALBION

HOW OLD WAS KENNY DALGLISH WHEN HE BECAME LIVERPOOL MANAGER IN 1985?

A.   32

B.   35

C.   34

WHICH TEAM HAS CONCEDED THE MOST OWN-GOALS AGAINST LIVERPOOL?

A.   MANCHESTER CITY

B.   TOTTENHAM

C.   EVERTON

THIS PLAYER DID NOT SCORE ON HIS PREMIER LEAGUE DEBUT FOR LIVERPOOL

A.   STAN COLLYMORE

B.   VICTOR MOSES

C.   FERNANDO TORRES

WHO WAS LIVERPOOL'S KIT MANUFACTURER IN THE 1996/1997 SEASON?

A.   PUMA

B.   ADIDAS

C.   NIKE

STANDARD CHARTERED REPLACED CARLSBERG AS LIVERPOOL'S PREMIER LEAGUE SHIRT SPONSORS IN;

A.   2010

B.   2014

C.   2009

THIS PLAYER DID NOT SCORE ON HIS BIRTHDAY FOR LIVERPOOL

A.   DANIEL STURRIDGE

B.   PETER CROUCH

C.   STEVEN GERRARD

HOW MANY PLAYERS HAVE TURNED OUT FOR BOTH LIVERPOOL AND EVERTON IN THEIR CAREER?

A.   1

B.   2

C.   5

ONE OF THESE HAS NOT TURNED FOR BOTH EVERTON AND LIVERPOOL

A.   JIM BEGLIN

B.   SANDER WESTERVEID

C.   PETER BEARDSLEY

NEXT TO ENGLAND, WHICH NATION HAS THE MOST LIVERPOOL PLAYERS?

A.   SCOTLAND

B.   SPAIN

C.   FRANCE

HOW MANY FRENCH PLAYERS HAVE TURNED OUT FOR LIVERPOOL?

A.   13

B.   20

C.   25

WHICH AFRICAN COUNTRY HAS PRODUCED THE MOST LIVERPOOL PLAYERS REPRESENTED?

A.   EGYPT

B.   SENEGAL

C.   SOUTH AFRICA

THIS SOUTH AMERICAN COUNTRY HAS PRODUCED THE MOST LIVERPOOL PLAYERS

A.   ARGENTINA

B.   BRAZIL

C.   URUGUAY

WHICH TEAM HAS CONCEDED THE MOST GOALS AGAINST LIVERPOOL IN THE PREMIER LEAGUE?

A.   ARSENAL

B.   NEWCASTLE

C.   EVERTON

WHICH TEAM DID LIVERPOOL KNOCK OUT IN 2016 TO REACH THE EUROPA LEAGUE SEMI-FINAL?

A.   CHELSEA

B.   BORUSSIA DORTMUND

C.   MANCHESTER UNITED

HOW MANY PREMIER LEAGUE GOALS DID FERNANDO TORRES SCORE IN HIS FIRST SEASON AT LIVERPOOL?

A.   24

B.   30

C.   27

WHO SCORED THE DECISIVE THIRD GOAL IN ISTANBUL 2005 CHAMPIONS LEAGUE FINAL?

A.   VLADMIR SMICER

B.   LUIS GARCIA

C.   STEVEN GERRARD

AGAINST WHICH TEAM DID SADIO MANE GET HIS FIRST LIVERPOOL HAT-TRICK

A.   SWANSEA

B.   PORTO

C.   MAN CITY

WHICH TEAM HAS RECEIVED THE MOST RED CARDS AGAINST LIVERPOOL?

A.   NEWCASTLE UNITED

B.   CHELSEA

C.   EVERTON

WHICH REFEREE HAS SENT OFF LIVERPOOL PLAYERS THE MOST?

A.   MARTIN ATKINSON

B.   GRAHAM POLL

C.   JONATHAN MOSS

WHO IS THE ONLY PLAYER TO SCORE THREE CONSECUTIVE HAT TRICKS FOR LIVERPOOL?

A.   IAN RUSH

B.   JACK BALMER

C.   LUIS SUAREZ

THE ONLY LIVERPOOL PLAYER TO SCORE HAT TRICKS IN SIX DIFFERENT COMPETITIONS

A.   JACK BALMER

B.   ROBBIE FOWLER

C.   IAN RUSH

PLAYER TO SCORE FOR LIVERPOOL IN 16 STRAIGHT SEASONS.

A.   STEVEN GERRARD

B.   IAN RUSH

C.   KENNY DALGLISH

HOW MANY OWN GOALS DID JAMIE CARRAGHER SCORE IN HIS ENTIRE LIVERPOOL CAREER?

A.   6

B.   7

C.   9

THREE LIVERPOOL PLAYERS HAVE GONE 200 GAMES WITHOUT SCORING A GOAL.

A.   RON YATES

B.   EPH LONGWORTH

C.   JAMIE CARRAGHER

NAME THE ONLY PLAYER TO SCORE HIS ONLY GOAL FOR LIVERPOOL IN A FINAL

A.   VLADIMER SMICER

B.   LUCAS LEIVA

C.   ANTONIO NUNEZ

THE FIRST REDS PLAYER TO SCORE IN TWO DIFFERENT FA CUP FINALS

A.   STEVEN GERRARD

B.   STEVE HEIGHWAY

C.   DJIBRIL CISSÉ

HOW MANY GOALS DID LUCAS LEIVA SCORE FOR LIVERPOOL?

A.   10

B.   7

C.   4

WHAT WAS LIVERPOOL'S FIRST EVER FA CUP RESULT?

A.   4-0 AGAINST NANTWICH IN 1892

B.   3-0 AGAINST EVERTON IN 1893

C.   4-5 AGAINST BLACKBURN IN 1900

RECORD CONSECUTIVE MATCHES WITHOUT CONCEDING A GOAL:

A.   18

B.   11

C.   12

MOST HOME WINS IN A SEASON IN ALL COMPETITIONS

A.   25

B.   19

C.   22

RECORD DEFEAT AT ANFIELD

A.   0-7

B.   0-9

C.   0-6

THE MOST ASSIST IN THE
2017/2018 SEASON

A.   TRENT ARNOLD

B.   ROBERTO FIRMINO

C.   MOHAMMED SALAH

HOW MANY GOALS DID LIVERPOOL SCORE IN THE 2010/2010 PL SEASON?

A.   61

B.   46

C.   18

WHICH PLAYER HAS THE MOST CONSECUTIVE APPEARANCES FOR LIVERPOOL

A.   RON YATES

B.   PHIL NEAL

C.   STEVE NICOL

QUESTION 109

MOST GAMES WITHOUT SCORING FOR AN OUTFIELD PLAYER

A.   EPHRAIM LONGWORTH,

B.   RON YATES

C.   PHIL NEAL

QUESTION 110

HOW OLD WAS NED DOIG WHEN HE LAST TURNED OUT FOR LIVERPOOL'S FIRST TEAM?

A.   39 YEARS

B.   35 YEARS

C.   41 YEARS

WHO SCORED THE MOST GOALS FOR LIVERPOOL IN THE 1985/1986 SEASON?

A.   IAN RUSH

B.   JAN MOLBY

C.   KENNY DALGLISH

WHICH OF THESE MANAGERS HAVE A BETTER WIN RATE IN EUROPE FOR LIVERPOOL?

A.   RAFA BENITEZ

B.   JOE FAGAN

C.   JURGEN KLOPP

HOW MANY PL GOALS DID LIVERPOOL SCORE IN THEIR TITLE-WINNING 2019-2020 SEASON?

A.   85.

B.   100

C.   79

114.WHO IS LIVERPOOL'S YOUNGEST FIRST-TEAM DEBUTANT IN A COMPETITIVE MATCH?

A.   JEROME SINCLAIR

B.   BEN WOODBURN

C.   HARVEY ELLIOT

HOW MANY TIMES WAS STEVEN GERRARD SENT-OFF IN THE LEAGUE AGAINST EVERTON?

A.   4

B.   2

C.   3

HOW OLD WAS NED DOIG WHEN HE MADE HIS LIVERPOOL DEBUT?

A.   37 YEARS AND 307 DAYS

B.   39 YEARS AND 44 DAYS

C.   36 YEARS AND 4 DAYS

PHIL NEAL PLAYED EVERY MINUTE OF EVERY LEAGUE AND CUP GAME FOR HOW MANY SEASONS?

A.   10 SEASONS

B.   7 SEASONS

C.   9 SEASONS

WHO HAS THE MOST TOP-FLIGHT LEAGUE GOALS IN A SEASON?

A.   MOHAMED SALAH

B.   GORDON HODGSON,

C.   IAN RUSH

WHO HAS SCORED IN THE MOST GAMES IN A SINGLE CAMPAIGN IN THE LEAGUE?

A.   MOHAMED SALAH

B.   IAN RUSH

C.   ROBBIE FOWLER

LIVERPOOL PLAYER WITH THE MOST HAT TRICK

A.   GORDON HODGSON

B.   IAN RUSH

C.   KENNY DALGLISH

HOW MANY GOALS DID DAVID FAIRCLOUGH SCORE AS A SUBSTITUTE?

A.   23

B.   19

C.   18

FASTEST LIVERPOOL PLAYER TO REACH 50 LEAGUE GOALS

A.   IAN RUSH

B.   MOHAMED SALAH

C.   FERNANDO TORRES

WHAT WAS FERNANDO TORRES NICKNAME AT LIVERPOOL?

A.   EL CUCO CABRA

B.   EL PIBO

C.   EL NINO

ONE OF THIS IS THE FIRST NON-BRITISH LIVERPOOL PLAYER TO WIN THE WORLD CUP

A.   XABI ALONSO

B.   ALLISON BECKER

C.   ABEL XAVIER

WHICH TROPHY DID GERRARD FIRST WIN AT LIVERPOOL?

A.   CHAMPIONS LEAGUE

B.   LEAGUE CUP.

C.   UEFA CUP

WHO WAS THE FIRST FOREIGN PLAYER TO REPRESENT LFC?

A.   DOUG RUDHAM

B.   AVI COHEN

C.   HOWARD GAYLE

HOW MANY HAT-TRICKS DID STEVEN GERRARD SCORE FOR LIVERPOOL

A.   6

B.   7

C.   5

WHICH PLAYER SCORED THE MOST GOALS FOR LIVERPOOL IN THE 1989/90 LEAGUE SEASON?

A.   PETER BEARDSLEY

B.   JOHN BARNES

C.   MICHAEL OWEN

WHICH PLAYER HAS THE MOST ASSIST IN EUROPE IN A SINGLE SEASON FOR LIVERPOOL?

A.   ROBERTO FIRMINO

B.   STEVEN GERRARD

C.   JAMES MILNER

PLAYER THAT HAS FACED LIVERPOOL MOST IN THE PL ERA?

A.   FRANK LAMPARD

B.   RYAN GIGGS

C.   GARETH BARRY

MOST GOALS FOR LIVERPOOL IN THE PREMIER LEAGUE

A.   IAN RUSH

B.   ROBBIE FOWLER

C.   LUIS SUAREZ

WHO WAS LIVERPOOL'S FIRST EVER OPPONENT IN THE PREMIER LEAGUE ERA?

A.   IPSWICH

B.   NOTTINGHAM FOREST

C.   ARSENAL

WHICH PLAYER WORE THE NO. 8 SHIRT BEFORE GERRARD?

A.   EMILE HESKEY

B.   JAMIE REDKNAPP

C.   TOMMY LEE

AGAINST WHICH SIDE DID STEVEN GERRARD FIRST WEAR THE CAPTAIN ARMBAND

A.   SOUTHAMPTON

B.   BASEL

C.   EVERTON

WHICH OF THESE PLAYERS HAS THE MOST PL HAT-TRICKS?

A.   LUIS SUAREZ

B.   MICHAEL OWEN

C.   STEVEN GERRARD

HOW MANY TIMES HAVE LIVERPOOL HAD TWO PLAYERS IN SENT OFF IN THE SAME GAME?

A.   3

B.   4

C.   6

LIVERPOOL HAVE NOT LOST TO THIS TEAM IN THE PREMIER LEAGUE

A.   READING

B.   BRIGHTON

C.   BARNSLEY

THIS PLAYER HAS NOT HAVE WORN THE NUMBER 18 SHIRT AT LIVERPOOL

A.   STEWART DOWNING

B.   ALBERTO MORENO

C.   TAKUMI MINAMINO

HOW MANY DRAWS
DID BILL SHANKLY?

A.   400

B.   302

C.   198

CAN YOU GUESS HOW MANY WINS
BILL SHANKLY ACQUIRED
AS LIVERPOOL MANAGER?

A.   903

B.   678

C.   783

WHO HAS MADE THE MOST APPEARANCES FOR LIVERPOOL IN EUROPE?

A.   STEVEN GERRARD

B.   JAMIE CARRAGHER

C.   STEVE NICOL

WHICH LIVERPOOL PLAYER HAS THE MOST INTERNATIONAL CAPS WHILE A LIVERPOOL PLAYER?

A.   STEVEN GERRARD

B.   FERNANDO TORRES

C.   XABI ALONSO

WHO IS FIRST NON-BRITISH PLAYER TO APPEAR IN A WORLD CUP FINAL?

A.   STEVE FINNAN

B.   DIETMAR HAMANN,

C.   XABI ALONSO

WHICH LIVERPOOL PLAYER HAS THE MOST PLAYER OF THE MONTH AWARDS IN THE PREMIER LEAGUE?

A.   STEVEN GERRARD

B.   LUIS SAUREZ

C.   SADIO MANE

WHAT IS THE MOST WINS AWAY FROM HOME THAT LIVERPOOL HAVE HAD IN A PL SEASON?

A.   12

B.   14

C.   9

WHAT IS THE RECORD CONSECUTIVE WINS LIVERPOOL HAVE HAD IN THE LEAGUE?

A.   11

B.   16

C.   18

WHAT IS THE RECORD CONSECUTIVE LEAGUE WINS FROM START OF SEASON FOR LIVERPOOL?

A.   23

B.   8

C.   18

WHO IS THE YOUNGEST GOAL SCORER FOR LIVERPOOL IN A COMPETITIVE GAME?

A.   HARVEY ELLIOT

B.   JACK ROBINSON

C.   BEN WOODBURN

WHAT IS THE RECORD CONSECUTIVE DEFEATS FOR LIVERPOOL?

A.   9

B.   12

C.   10

FIRST SPANISH LIVERPOOL PLAYER

A.   ANTONIO NUNEZ

B.   ALBERT ORTEGA

C.   DIDI HAMMAN

AGAINST WHAT SIDE DID STEVEN GERRARD MAKE HIS COMPETITIVE DEBUT

A.   MANCHESTER UNITED

B.   BLACKBURN ROVERS

C.   EVERTON

WHAT IS LONGEST UNBEATEN RUN FOR LIVERPOOL IN THE LEAGUE

A.   50

B.   41

C.   44

WHAT IS THE RECORD FOR THE CONSECUTIVE DRAWS?

A.   11

B.   6

C.   3

WHICH PLAYER MADE THE MOST WORLD CUP APPEARANCES AS A LIVERPOOL PLAYER?

A.   XABI ALONSO

B.   JOHN BARNES

C.   STEVEN GERRARD

WHAT IS THE RECORD LEAGUE DEFEATS IN A SEASON FOR LIVERPOOL?

A.   23

B.   21

C.   19

WHAT IS THE FEWEST NUMBER OF LEAGUE WINS IN A SEASON FOR LIVERPOOL?

A.   2 WINS

B.   6 WINS

C.   12 WINS

QUESTION 157

WHICH BAND RELEASED YNWA ANTHEM SUNG BY LIVERPOOL FANS?

A.   THE BEATLES

B.   GERRY AND THE PACEMAKERS

C.   PINK FLOYD

QUESTION 158

WHEN WAS YNWA ANTHEM FIRST SUNG BY LIVERPOOL SUPPORTERS?

A.   1977

B.   1963

C.   1965

WHICH OF THIS CELEBRITY IS A LIVERPOOL FAN?

A.   DANIEL CRAIG

B.   LIAM GALLAGHER

C.   MEGAN FOX

WHAT IS KENNY DALGLISH'S MIDDLE NAME?

A.   NOBERT

B.   MATHIESON

C.   BRAINARD

WHICH OF THESE PLAYER WON BALON D'OR AS A LIVERPOOL PLAYER?

A.   EMILE HESKEY

B.   MICHAEL OWEN

C.   STEVE MCMANAMAN

WHICH OVERSEA LIVERPOOL PLAYER HAS MADE THE MOST APPEARANCES FOR LIVERPOOL?

A.   SADIO MANE

B.   LUCAS LEIVA

C.   BRUCE GROBBELAAR

WHO WAS LIVERPOOL'S TOP SCORER IN 2001/2002 SEASON?

A.   EMILE HESKEY

B.   MICHAEL OWEN

C.   PHIL THOMPSON

BIGGEST STAND IN ANFIELD BY CAPACITY

A.   MAIN STAND

B.   STEVEN GERRARD STAND

C.   PARK LANE STAND

PLAYER TO SCORE THE MOST ON NEW YEAR'S DAY. TIP IS SCORED IN SEVEN NEW-YEAR'S DAYS

A.   IAN RUSH

B.   ANDY CARROL

C.   OXLADE CHAMBERLAIN

HOW MANY YELLOW CARDS DID VAN DJIK RECEIVE IN PREMIER LEAGUE 2018/2019 SEASON?

A.   3

B.   1

C.   5

QUESTION 167

WHICH STAND IS THE SMALLEST AT ANFIELD BY CAPACITY?

A.   SPION KOP STAND

B.   SIR KENNY DALGLISH STAND

C.   ANFIELD ROAD END

QUESTION 168

NAME OF LIVERPOOL FIRST OWNER

A.   NICK POWELL

B.   JOHN HOULDING

C.   TOM HENRY

WHAT WAS THE SIR DALGLISH STAND CALLED BEFORE?

A.   CENTENARY STAND

B.   KOP END

C.   HILLSBOROUGH TOWER

WHO HAS THE MOST APPEARANCES FOR LIVERPOOL AMONG THESE PLAYERS?

A.   LUCAS LEIVA

B.   JOHN ARNE RIISE

C.   MARTIN SKRTEL

WHO PLAYED MOST MATCHES FOR LIVERPOOL?

A.   STEVEN GERRARD

B.   RAY CLEMENCE

C.   KENNY DALGLISH

WHICH LIVERPOOL PLAYER FAMOUSLY TATTOOED YNWA ON HIS KNUCKLES?

A.   DANIEL AGGER

B.   ROBERTO FIRMINO

C.   MARTIN SKRTEL

THE STRIKER WITH THE MOST GAMES FOR LIVERPOOL

A.   JOHN BARNES

B.   IAN RUSH

C.   ROBBIE FOWLER

LFC FIRST BLACK PLAYER

A.   JOHN BARNES

B.   SALIF DIOA

C.   HOWARD GAYLE

LIVERPOOL CAPTAIN WITH THE MOST APPEARANCE

A.   TOM YATES

B.   JOHN BARNES

C.   STEVEN GERRARD

APART FROM NABY KEITA, WHICH OTHER GUINEAN HAS FEATURED FOR LIVERPOOL?

A.   EL HADJI DIOUF

B.   SINAMA PONGOLLE

C.   TITI CAMARA

HOW MANY GOALS DID KUYT SCORE IN THE PL FOR LIVERPOOL?

A.   101

B.   51

C.   66

LAST PLAYER TO SCORE FOR BRENDAN RODGERS BEFORE HE WAS SACKED AS LIVERPOOL MANAGER

A.   DANNY INGS

B.   CHRISTIAN BENTEKE

C.   ROBERTO FIRMINO

FIRST ROBERTO FIRMINO GOAL FOR LIVERPOOL CAME AGAINST

A.   ARSENAL

B.   MANCHESTER CITY

C.   LEICESTER CITY

FIRST BELGIAN TO PLAY FOR LIVERPOOL

A.   CHRISTIAN BENTEKE

B.   SIMON MIGNOLET

C.   DIVOCK ORIGI

HOW MANY FULL-TIME MANAGERS HAVE LIVERPOOL HAD?

A.   25

B.   24

C.   21

SPANIARD WITH MOST GOALS FOR LIVERPOOL

A.   XABI ALONSO

B.   FERNADO TORRES

C.   RAUL MEIRELES

WHAT YEAR WAS THE FIRST MATCH PLAYED AT ANFIELD?

A.   1896

B.   1888

C.   1893

ONE THESE PLAYERS CAPTAINED LIVERPOOL MORE THAN ONCE IN THE PREMIER LEAGUE

A.   EMRE CAN

B.   JON FLANAGAN

C.   DIRK KUYT

WHICH SIDE HAS SCORED THE MOST SPOT KICKS AGAINST LIVERPOOL?

A.   MANCHESTER UNITED

B.   TOTTENHAM MANCHESTER CITY

C.   LEEDS UNITED

WHO SCORED LIVERPOOL'S 50TH AWAY GOAL IN THE UEFA CHAMPIONS LEAGUE?

A.   EMRE CAN

B.   JON FLANAGAN

C.   DIRK KUYT

WHO SCORED LIVERPOOL'S 50TH HOME GOAL IN THE UEFA CHAMPIONS LEAGUE:

A.   PETER CROUCH

B.   CRAIG BELLAMY

C.   RYAN BABEL

LIVERPOOL'S BIGGEST LAST DAY WIN IN THE PREMIER LEAGUE

A.   5-0 IPSWICH TOWN

B.   6-1 STOCK

C.   6-2 TOTTENHAM

BIGGEST LAST DAY LOSS
IN THE PREMIER LEAGUE

A.   5-0 TOTTENHAM

B.   6-1 AGAINST STOKE

C.   4-0 ARSENAL

ONLY PLAYER TO RECEIVE A RED CARD
ON THE LAST DAY OF THE PREMIER
LEAGUE SEASON FOR LIVERPOOL

A.   LUIS SUAREZ

B.   ALBERTO MORENO

C.   STEVEN GERRARD

WHO SCORED LIVERPOOL'S 1000TH GOAL AT ANFIELD IN THE PL

A.   ADAM LALLANA

B.   ROBERTO FIRMINO

C.   RICKIE LAMBERT

WHAT IS JURGEN KLOPP'S MIDDLE NAME?

A.   ULLA

B.   ALBERT

C.   NOBERT

WHAT IS JORDAN HENDERSON'S MIDDLE NAME?

A.   BRIAN

B.   NOBERT

C.   JAMES

WHO SCORED LIVERPOOL'S 10,000TH GOAL IN ALL COMPETITIONS?

A.   DIVOCK ORIGI

B.   DIOGO JOTA

C.   GEORGINIO WIJNALDUM

WHO SCORED FIRST ANFIELD GOAL FOR LIVERPOOL?

A.   JIMMY SMITH

B.   AVI COHEN

C.   JOCK SMITH

ONE OF THIS IS NOT A STAND AT ANFIELD?

A.   MAIN STAND

B.   SPION KOP STAND

C.   SHANKLY STAND

QUESTION 197

THE TWO GATES AT ANFIELD ARE NAMED AFTER

A.   TWO LIVERPOOL COACHES

B.   TWO LIVERPOOL OWNERS

C.   TWO ENGLISH POETS

QUESTION 198

WHAT TEAM WAS LIVERPOOL PLAYING DURING THE HILLSBOROUGH DISASTER?

A.   LEEDS UNITED

B.   NOTTINGHAM FOREST

C.   SHEFFIELD UNITED

HOW MANY FATALITIES WERE RECORDED IN THE HILLSBOROUGH DISASTER?

A.   TWO LIVERPOOL COACHES

B.   TWO LIVERPOOL OWNERS

C.   TWO ENGLISH POETS

AGAINST WHICH TEAM DID LIVERPOOL BEGIN THEIR 2018/2019 CHAMPIONS LEAGUE CAMPAIGN?

A.   RED STAR BELGRADE

B.   PSG

C.   NAPOLI

WHO SCORED ONE AND ASSISTED ANOTHER IN LIVERPOOL'S QUARTER FINAL MATCH IN THE 2018/2019 CHAMPIONS LEAGUE SEASON?

A.   SADIO MANE

B.   VIRGIL VAN DJIK

C.   DIVOCK ORIGI

HOW MANY SECONDS SEPARATED GEORGINIO WIJNALDUM'S GOAL AGAINST BARCELONA IN THE SEMI-FINAL?

A.   122

B.   102

C.   200

WHICH TEAM DID LIVERPOOL BEAT IN THE 1984 EUROPEAN CUP FINAL?

A.   INTER MILAN

B.   AC MILAN

C.   ROMA

WHEN DID LIVERPOOL WIN THEIR FIRST FA CUP?

A.   1892

B.   1894

C.   1890

WHICH ROAD RUNS BEHIND THE KOP STAND AT ANFIELD?

A.   KOP ROAD

B.   STANLEY PARK ROAD

C.   WALTON BRECK ROAD

WHICH TEAM DID LIVERPOOL PLAY FIRST IN THEIR FIRST PREMIER LEAGUE WINNING SEASON?

A.   NORWICH CITY

B.   CRYSTAL PALACE

C.   WATFORD

ANSWERS

#	Ans	#	Ans	#	Ans	#	Ans
1.	B.	53.	C	105.	C	157.	B
2.	C.	54.	A	106.	B	158.	C
3.	A.	55.	C	107.	A	159.	C
4.	B.	56.	B	108.	B	160.	B
5.	A.	57.	A.	109.	A	161.	B
6.	C.	58.	B	110.	C	162.	C
7.	A	59.	A	111.	A	163.	B
8.	C	60.	C	112.	B	164.	A
9.	B	61.	C	113.	A	165.	A
10.	A	62.	B	114.	A	166.	B
11.	C	63.	C	115.	B	167.	C
12.	B	64.	B	116.	A	168.	B
13.	C	65.	B	117.	C	169.	A
14.	A	66.	A	118.	B	170.	B
15.	B	67.	C	119.	A	171.	A
16.	A	68.	C	120.	A	172.	A
17.	C	69.	A	121.	C	173.	B
18.	A	70.	C	122.	B	174.	C
19.	C	71.	B	123.	C	175.	C
20.	B	72.	C	124.	A	176.	C
21.	B	73.	A	125.	B	177.	B
22.	C	74.	A	126.	A	178.	A
23.	B	75.	C	127.	C	179.	B
24.	A	76.	B	128.	B	180.	B
25.	B	77.	C	129.	C	181.	C
26.	A	78.	B	130.	B	182.	B
27.	C	79.	A	131.	B	183.	C
28.	B	80.	C	132.	B	184.	A
29.	C	81.	C	133.	A	185.	A
30.	C	82.	A	134.	A	186.	B
31.	A	83.	B	135.	B	187.	A
32.	A	84.	A	136.	B	188.	A
33.	A	85.	B	137.	B	189.	B
34.	B	86.	B	138.	A	190.	C
35.	A	87.	B	139.	C	191.	C
36.	B	88.	C	140.	C	192.	C
37.	B	89.	A	141.	B	193.	A
38.	C.	90.	A	142.	A	194.	B
39.	C.	91.	B	143.	B	195.	C
40.	A	92.	C	144.	A	196.	C
41.	A	93.	A	145.	B	197.	A
42.	C	94.	B	146.	C	198.	B
43.	A	95.	C	147.	C	199.	B
44.	B	96.	A	148.	C	200.	B
45.	C	97.	B	149.	A	201.	B
46.	A	98.	B	150.	B	202.	A
47.	C	99.	C	151.	B	203.	C
48.	A	100.	B	152.	C	204.	A
49.	A	101.	B	153.	B	205.	C
50.	C	102.	A	154.	C	206.	A
51.	A	103.	B	155.	A		
52.	A	104.	C	156.	A		

NOTES

NOTES

NOTES

NOTES

NOTES

NOTES

NOTES

NOTES

NOTES

Printed in Great Britain
by Amazon

13180288R00071